SQL Data Analysis for Beginners

How to Learn SQL in Less Than One Week. The Ultimate Step-by-Step Complete Course from Novice to Advance Programmer

William Brown

The information in the following pages is broadly considered a truthful and accurate account of facts and as such, any inattention, use, or misuse of the information in question by the reader will render any resulting actions solely under their purview. There are no scenarios in which the publisher or the original author of this work can be in any fashion deemed liable for any hardship or damages that may befall them after undertaking information described herein.

Additionally, the information in the following pages is intended only for informational purposes and should thus be thought of as universal. As befitting its nature, it is presented without assurance regarding its prolonged validity or interim quality. Trademarks that are mentioned are done without written consent and can in no way be considered an endorsement from the trademark holder.

Table of contents

Introduction

Data is the foundation of today's businesses. Enterprise computing represents the pinnacle of data-driven enterprises. The significance of organized data storage is undeniably in the spotlight. And, at a time when the computing paradigm is gradually moving to the cloud and storage costs are rapidly declining, companies are increasingly relying on data to fine-tune their operations. It is, therefore, important to have a fundamental understanding of this hierarchical model of data storage and retrieval.

On the other hand, a beginner is bound to feel lost in the vast amount of knowledge available in the wild. This book, a guide to SQL, comes to the rescue by beginning at the very foundation of SQL — the very fabric — and working up to the bigger picture from there. The SQL definition has been around for over four decades. It has, however, evolved and continues to evolve. We've all learned SQL at some stage during our schooling. We're here to improve things by getting away from antiquated technologies and procedures. When you study a method using ancient methods and practices, you must assimilate it and reconsider its implementation in the modern industry until you become a part of it. On the other hand, with this book, you can learn the concepts using common tools and practices.

Without SQL, data management and database administration are incomplete. Understanding the fundamentals of SQL, which will take you a long way in your career, is needed to feel relaxed using the powerful SQL as part of your administration or production. As a result, in this book, we begin with an introduction to SQL and then understand SQL Server's key features. Starting with SQL standards and progressing to building tables, recognizing and defining relationships, writing Transact-SQL commands, and so on, the chapters will walk you through the internal workings of SQL.

Chapter 1: What Is SQL?

SQL is known as Structured Query Language. SQL is a language for interacting with databases. It is the basic language for management systems of relational database, according to ANSI (American National Standards Institute). Scripts are used to execute activities including updating data in a database and retrieving data from one. Oracle, Microsoft SQL Server, Sybase, Access, Ingres, and other management systems of relational database that use SQL are only a few examples. While most relational databases use SQL, they also get their own proprietary plugins that are only available on their own platform. Standard Sql statements such as "Delete," "Select," "Insert," "Create," "Update," and "Down" may be used to do almost everything about a database.

SQL is a database management language that allows you to create, delete, retrieve, and modify data in databases. While SQL is an ANSI (American National Standards Institute) standard language, there are several SQL variants.

The Relational Database System (RDBMS) standard language is SQL. SQL is the standard database language used by all

Management systemsof relational database (RDMS) such as Sybase, MySQL, Oracle, MS Access, Informix, Postgres, and SQL Server.

Also, they are utilizing different languages, such as −

- MS Access version of SQL = JET SQL etc.

- MS SQL Server = T-SQL,

- Oracle = PL/SQL,

1.1 Why SQL?

SQL is commonly used because it has the following benefits:

- It allows operators to view data stored in management systems of relational database.

- Allows operators to provide a description of the results.

- Allows operators to identify and modify the data in a database.

- SQL plugins, libraries, and pre-compilers may be used to integrate within other languages.

- Provides operators with the ability to build and delete databases and tables.

- Allows operators to construct database views, stored procedures, and features.

- Permissions for tables, processes, and views may be configured by users.

1.2 A Brief History of SQL

- The founder of relational databases is IBM's Dr. Edgar F. "Ted" Codd, who founded it in 1970. He defined a database relational model.

- Structured Query Language debuted in 1974.

- In 1978, IBM worked to refine Codd's ideas and published the System/R product.

- In 1986, IBM created the first relational database prototype, which was standardized by ANSI. Relational Software, which later became known as Oracle, launched the first relational database.

Chapter 2 – How SQL Works?

2.1 SQL Process

When you run a SQL command against any RDBMS, the system figures out the best place to handle out your query and the SQL engine works out how to interpret it.

This procedure has a number of different elements.

These are –

- Query Dispatcher
- Classic Query Engine
- SQL Query Engine
- Optimization Engines, etc.

Non-SQL queries are handled by a classic database engine, but logical files are handled by a SQL query engine.

The SQL Architecture is depicted in the diagram below.

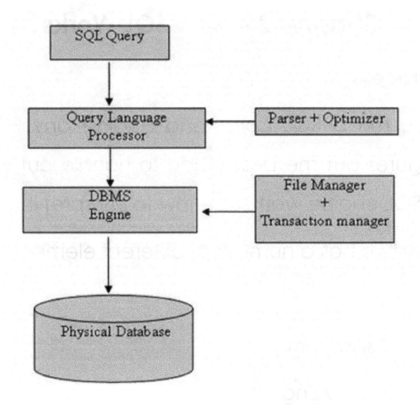

2.2 SQL Commands

The CREATE, UPDATE, INSERT, SELECT, DELETE, and DROP are the basic SQL commands for working with relational databases. Depending on their existence, these commands can be divided into the following categories:

Language of Data Definition - DDL

Sr. No.	Command & Description
1	**CREATE**

	Creates a new database table, overview of a table, or other entity.
2	**ALTER** Used to modify the selected object such as table
3	**DROP** Deletes a table in the database, overview of a table, or other entity.

Language of Data Manipulation - DML

Sr. No.	Command & Description
1	**SELECT** To retrieve specific records from the table.
2	**INSERT** Creation of record.
3	**UPDATE** To modify the record.

4	**DELETE** To delete the record.

Language of Data Control - DCL

Sr. No.	Command & Description
1	**GRANT** To give control to the user.
2	**REVOKE** To take back the control from the user.

2.3 SQL - RDBMS Concepts

What is the Management System of Relational Database?

Management System of Relational Database (RDBMS) is an acronym for Relational Database Management System. SQL and all modern database systems such as IBM DB2, MS SQL

Server, MySQL, Oracle, and Microsoft Access are built on top of RDBMS.

A management system of relational database (RDBMS) is a relational database (DBMS) that is built on E. F. Codd's relational model.

What is a table?

The data in a management system of relational database (RDBMS) is deposited in databank structures known as tables. This table, which has several columns and rows, is essentially a list of similar data entries.

Remember that the most popular and basic type of data storage in a relational database is a table. A CUSTOMERS table is shown in the following program.

```
+----+----------+-----+-----------+----------+
| ID | NAME     | AGE | ADDRESS   | SALARY   |
+----+----------+-----+-----------+----------+
|  1 | Ramesh   |  32 | Ahmedabad |  2000.00 |
|  2 | Khilan   |  25 | Delhi     |  1500.00 |
|  3 | kaushik  |  23 | Kota      |  2000.00 |
|  4 | Chaitali |  25 | Mumbai    |  6500.00 |
|  5 | Hardik   |  27 | Bhopal    |  8500.00 |
|  6 | Komal    |  22 | MP        |  4500.00 |
|  7 | Muffy    |  24 | Indore    | 10000.00 |
+----+----------+-----+-----------+----------+
```

What is a field?

Each table is divided into fields, which are smaller entities. NAME, ADDRESS, ID, AGE, and SALARY are the fields in the CUSTOMERS table.

A field is a table column that is used to store basic information about each record in the table.

What is a Record or a Row?

Each individual entry in a table is referred to as a record, also known as a row of records. In the CUSTOMERS table, for reference, there are seven reports. A single row of details or record from the CUSTOMERS table is seen below –

```
+----+----------+-----+-----------+----------+
| 1  | Ramesh   |  32 | Ahmedabad |  2000.00 |
+----+----------+-----+-----------+----------+
```

This table shows the horizontal entry of data.

What is a column?

In a table, a column is a vertical object that includes all information related to a particular area.

A column in the CUSTOMERS table, for example, is ADDRESS, which describes location summary and will look like this –

```
+------------+
| ADDRESS    |
+------------+
| Ahmedabad  |
| Delhi      |
| Kota       |
| Mumbai     |
| Bhopal     |
| MP         |
| Indore     |
+----+------+
```

What is a NULL value?

In a row, a NULL value is a value in an area that tends to be blank, implying that an area with a NULL value has no value.

It is important to consider the difference between a NULL value and a zero value or a field of spaces. An area with a NULL value has been left blank during the record production process.

SQL Constraints

Constraints are laws that are applied to data columns in a table. These are used to restrict the types of information that can be entered into a table. This means that the data in the system is accurate and reliable.

Constraints may be applied at the column or table level. Table level constraints are extended to the whole table, while column level constraints are only applied to one column.

The following are a few of the most widely used SQL restrictions.

- CHECK Constraint - guarantees that all values in a column meet those criteria.

- DEFAULT Constraint Sets a default value for the column if none is defined.

- FOREIGN KEY recognizes a row/record in some other database table in a unique way.

- INDEX – Used to easily generate and restore data from a database.

- The NOT NULL constraint prevents a column from having a NULL value.

- PRIMARY KEY distinguishes each row/record in a database table in a unique way.

- UNIQUE constraint ensures that any value in a column is unique.

2.4 SQL - RDBMS Databases

There is a variety of common RDBMS to choose from. This topic provides a high-level summary of some of the most widely used RDBMSs. This will allow you to compare their basic characteristics.

MySQL

MySQL is a Database system that is open-source created by MySQL AB, a Swedish corporation.

MySQL runs on a variety of operating systems, including Microsoft Windows, UNIX, Linux distributions, and Mac OS X. MySQL is available in both free and premium formats, based on the type of use (non-commercial vs. commercial) and functionality. MySQL includes a SQL database server that is extremely fast, multi-threaded, multi-user, and stable.

Features

- Comprehensive Application Development.

- High Availability.

- High Performance.

- Lowest Total Cost of Ownership.

- Management Ease.

- Open-Source Freedom and 24 x 7 Support.

- Robust Transactional Support.

- Scalability and Flexibility

- Run anything.

- Strong Data Protection.

- Data and Web Warehouse Strengths.

MS SQL Server

Microsoft SQL Server is a Relational Database (RDBMS) that was created by Microsoft Inc. Its most popular query languages are-

- ANSI SQL

- T-SQL

Features

- CLR integration

- Database Mail

- Database mirroring

- DDL triggers

- High Availability

- High Performance

- Ranking functions

- TRY...CATCH.

- Database snapshots

- Isolation levels Row version-based

- Service Broker

- XML integration

ORACLE

It is a multi-user domain management system for a wide number of users. Oracle is a relational database management system that was created by the 'Oracle Corporation.' Oracle strives to effectively control its tools, which include a record of information shared by various clients demanding and sending data through the network.

For server/client computing, it is an outstanding database server choice. Oracle supports all major operating systems, including NetWare, MSDOS, OS/2, UnixWare, and most UNIX flavors, for both clients and servers.

Features

- Analytic SQL

- ASM

- Bitmap indexes

- Concurrency

- Data mining

- Data Warehousing

- Locking Mechanisms

- Materialized views

- Parallel Execution

- Partitioning

- Portability

- Quiesce Database

- Read Consistency

- Resource Manager

- Scheduler

- Self-managing databank

- SQL*Plus

- Table compression

MS ACCESS

This is one of Microsoft's most famous products. Microsoft Access is an information administration program for beginners. For small-scale projects, the MS Microsoft access is not only affordable but also strong.

MS Access makes use of the Jet database engine, which has its own SQL dialect (sometimes referred to as Jet SQL). MS Access is included in the Microsoft Office Technical kit. MS Access provides an intuitive graphical interface that is easy to use.

Features

- Users can generate tables, forms, queries, and reports and use macros to link them together.

- Data can be imported and exported in a variety of formats, including Oracle, Excel, dBase, SQL Server, Outlook, ASCII, ODBC, FoxPro, and Paradox.

- The Jet Database format (ACCDB or MDB in Access 2007) will hold both the program and the data in a single disk. This makes it very easy to delegate the whole program to another person who can run it in remote locations.

- Parameterized queries are available in Microsoft Access. DAO or ADO may be used to reference these questions and Access tables from other programs such as VB6 and.NET.

- As an equivalent to the Jet Database Engine, Server desktop of Microsoft SQL editions can be used for Access.

Microsoft Access is a database that runs on a file server. Microsoft Access does not support database triggers, stored processes, or transaction logging, unlike client-server relational database.

2.5 SQL Syntax

The syntax is a series of standards and instructions that SQL adheres to. This guide provides a short introduction to SQL by outlining all of the major SQL syntaxes.

SQL Statements

SQL statements are similar to plain English in that they are simple and concise, but they have a special syntax. A SQL statement is made up of a series of keywords, identifiers, and other elements. All SQL statements begin with one of the following keywords: ALTER, SHOW, USE, CREATE, INSERT,

SELECT, DELETE, UPDATE, DROP and end with a semicolon (;).
An instance of a true SQL statement can be seen below.

```
1   SELECT emp_name, hire_date, salary FROM employees WHERE salary > 5000;
```

You may also compose the same sentence as follows for easier readability:

```
1   SELECT emp_name, hire_date, salary
2   FROM employees
3   WHERE salary > 5000;
```

When you use a semicolon at the closing of a SQL statement, it either ends the statement or sends it to the database. While certain information management systems do not have such a provision, it is considered best practice to do so.

SQL Case Sensitivity

Check out the following SQL statement for information retrieval from the employee's table:

```
1   SELECT emp_name, hire_date, salary FROM employees;
```

Following is another way to express the same idea:

```
1   select emp_name, hire_date, salary from employees;
```

Since SQL keywords are case-insensitive, select would be the same as SELECT. However, based on the operating system, database and table naming can be case-sensitive. Unix and Linux operating systems, generally, are case-sensitive; however, Windows systems are not. To make the SQL keywords stand out from the rest of the text in a SQL statement, it is best to write them in capital letters.

SQL Comments

A comment is basically text which the database system ignores. Comments may be used to give a brief description of the SQL statement.

Both single-line and multi-line comments are accepted by SQL. Begin each line with two back-to-back hyphens to create a single-line comment (--). Consider the following scenario:

```
1    -- Select all the employees
2    SELECT * FROM employees;
```

Furthermore, begin the multi-line comments with a slash accompanied by an asterisk (/*) and conclude with an asterisk accompanied by a slash (*/), as shown:

```
1    /* Select all the employees whose
2    salary is greater than 5000 */
3    SELECT * FROM employees
4    WHERE salary > 5000;
```

Various SQL Syntax

The MySQL server was used to verify all of the examples in this guide.

- SQL Statement "SELECT"

```
SELECT column1, column2....columnN
FROM   table_name;
```

- SQL Clause "DISTINCT"

```
SELECT DISTINCT column1, column2....columnN
FROM   table_name;
```

- SQL Clause "WHERE"

```
SELECT column1, column2....columnN
FROM   table_name
WHERE  CONDITION;
```

- SQL Clause "AND/OR"

```
SELECT column1, column2....columnN
FROM   table_name
WHERE  CONDITION-1 {AND|OR} CONDITION-2;
```

- SQL Clause "IN"

```
SELECT column1, column2....columnN
FROM   table_name
WHERE  column_name IN (val-1, val-2,...val-N);
```

- SQL Clause "BETWEEN"

```
SELECT column1, column2....columnN
FROM    table_name
WHERE   column_name BETWEEN val-1 AND val-2;
```

- SQL Clause "LIKE"

```
SELECT column1, column2....columnN
FROM    table_name
WHERE   column_name LIKE { PATTERN };
```

- SQL Clause "ORDER BY"

```
SELECT column1, column2....columnN
FROM    table_name
WHERE   CONDITION
ORDER BY column_name {ASC|DESC};
```

- SQL Clause "GROUP BY"

```
SELECT SUM(column_name)
FROM    table_name
WHERE   CONDITION
GROUP BY column_name;
```

- SQL Clause "COUNT"

```
SELECT COUNT(column_name)
FROM    table_name
WHERE   CONDITION;
```

- SQL Clause "HAVING"

```
SELECT SUM(column_name)
FROM    table_name
WHERE   CONDITION
GROUP BY column_name
HAVING (arithematic function condition);
```

- SQL Statement "CREATE TABLE"

```
CREATE TABLE table_name(
column1 datatype,
column2 datatype,
column3 datatype,
.....
columnN datatype,
PRIMARY KEY( one or more columns )
);
```

- SQL Statement "DROP TABLE"

```
DROP TABLE table_name;
```

- SQL Statement "CREATE INDEX"

```
CREATE UNIQUE INDEX index_name
ON table_name ( column1, column2,...columnN);
```

- SQL Statement "DROP INDEX"

```
ALTER TABLE table_name
DROP INDEX index_name;
```

- SQL Statement "DESC"

```
DESC table_name;
```

- SQL Statement "TRUNCATE TABLE"

```
TRUNCATE TABLE table_name;
```

- SQL Statement "ALTER TABLE"

```
ALTER TABLE table_name {ADD|DROP|MODIFY} column_name {data_ype};
```

- SQL Statement "ALTER TABLE" (Rename)

```
ALTER TABLE table_name RENAME TO new_table_name;
```

- SQL Statement "INSERT INTO"

```
INSERT INTO table_name( column1, column2....columnN)
VALUES ( value1, value2....valueN);
```

- SQL Statement "UPDATE"

```
UPDATE table_name
SET column1 = value1, column2 = value2....columnN=valueN
[ WHERE  CONDITION ];
```

- SQL Statement "DELETE"

```
DELETE FROM table_name
WHERE  {CONDITION};
```

- SQL Statement "CREATE DATABASE"

```
CREATE DATABASE database_name;
```

- SQL Statement "DROP DATABASE"

```
DROP DATABASE database_name;
```

- SQL Statement "USE"

```
USE database_name;
```

- SQL Statement "COMMIT"

```
COMMIT;
```

- SQL Statement "ROLLBACK"

```
ROLLBACK;
```

2.6 SQL Operators

What is an Operator in SQL?

An operator is a specified word or symbol that is used in the WHERE clause of a SQL statement to execute operations like arithmetic and comparison operations. These Operators are also used to define conditions in SQL statements and to function as conjunctions for several conditions in a single statement.

- Logical operators

- Comparison operators

- Operators used to negate conditions.

- Arithmetic operators

SQL Arithmetic Operators

If 'variable a' has a value of 10 and 'variable b' has a value of 20, then –

Operator	Description	Example
+ (Addition)	Adds values on either side of the operator.	a + b will give 30
- (Subtraction)	Subtracts right hand operand from left hand operand.	a - b will give -10
* (Multiplication)	Multiplies values on either side of the operator.	a * b will give 200
/ (Division)	Divides left hand operand by right hand operand.	b / a will give 2
% (Modulus)	Divides left hand operand by right hand operand and returns remainder.	b % a will give 0

SQL Comparison Operators

If 'variable a' has a value of 10 and 'variable b' has a value of 20, then –

Operator	Description	Example
=	Checks if the values of two operands are equal or not, if yes then condition becomes true.	(a = b) is not true.
!=	Checks if the values of two operands are equal or not, if values are not equal then condition becomes true.	(a != b) is true.
<>	Checks if the values of two operands are equal or not, if values are not equal then condition becomes true.	(a <> b) is true.
>	Checks if the value of left operand is greater than the value of right operand, if yes then condition becomes true.	(a > b) is not true.
<	Checks if the value of left operand is less than the value of right operand, if yes then condition becomes true.	(a < b) is true.
>=	Checks if the value of left operand is greater than or equal to the value of right operand, if yes then condition becomes true.	(a >= b) is not true.
<=	Checks if the value of left operand is less than or equal to the value of right operand, if yes then condition becomes true.	(a <= b) is true.
!<	Checks if the value of left operand is not less than the value of right operand, if yes then condition becomes true.	(a !< b) is false.
!>	Checks if the value of left operand is not greater than the value of right operand, if yes then condition becomes true.	(a !> b) is true.

SQL Logical Operators

The following list consists of all logical operators included in SQL:

- **ALL**

When a value is compared to all of the values in some other value set, the ALL operator is used.

- **AND**

The AND operator enables several conditions to occur in the **WHERE clause** of a SQL statement.

- **ANY**

The ANY operator compares a value to any valid value within the list according to the condition.

- **BETWEEN**

The BETWEEN operator helps find the values that are between the minimum and maximum values in a series of given values.

- **EXISTS**

The EXISTS operator helps check for a row in a given table that matches a certain set of criteria.

- **IN**

Where a value is compared to a set of specific values that have been defined, the IN operator is used.

- **LIKE**

The LIKE operator compares a value to other values that are identical using wildcard operators.

- **NOT**

The NOT operator switches the sense of the logical operator it is used with. For example, NOT IN, NOT BETWEEN, NOT EXISTS, and so on. It is a negation operator.

- **OR**

The WHERE clause of a SQL statement uses OR operator to join several conditions.

- **IS NULL**

When a number is compared to a NULL value, the NULL operator is used.

- **UNIQUE**

The UNIQUE operator looks for uniqueness in every row of a table (without duplicates).

Chapter 3 – Basic Rules and Practical Application

As you already know, SQL is used to work with databases, but you will need access to a database server before you can begin playing with SQL.

Using the online SQL editor, you can evaluate or execute any SQL statements used as examples in this guide. On the client-side, the SQL editor includes A web SQL Database to store and manipulate data. To execute any SQL statements, though, you'll need access to a full-featured database management system such as SQL Server, MySQL, or something similar.

3.1 Database Example for Basic Statements

A dataset from the bike-sharing company is used in this context, containing data on over 1.5 million trips taken with the service.

Let's begin by looking at the database. There are two tables in the database: trips and stations. First, let's have a look at the trip chart. The following columns are included:

- bike number — The trip's exclusive Hubway code for the bike.

- Year of birth — The user's year of birth (only for registered members).

- Length — The time it takes to travel, estimated in seconds.

- End date — The day and date that the journey came to an end.

- Endstation — The 'id' of the station where the journey came to an end.

- Sex — The user's gender (only for registered members).

- Id — Each trip is identified by a specific integer that acts as a reference.

- Start date — The start date and time of the journey.

- Start station — An integer that correlates to the station's id column in the station's table.

- Subtype — The user's subscription class. Those with membership are labeled "Registered," while those without a membership are labeled "Casual."

- Zip code — The user's zip code (only for registered members).

Here are some questions we'll try to answer throughout this section using this knowledge and the SQL commands we'll learn shortly:

- Do licensed or occasional users travel for longer periods?

- How long did the average travel take?

- How long do people above the age of 30 spend on average on their trips?

- How many journeys have 'registered' people taken?

- What was the longest trip's duration?

- Which bike did the most trips on?

To answer these questions, we'll use the following SQL commands:

- AND

- AVG

- COUNT

- GROUP BY

- LIMIT

- MAX

- MIN

- OR

- ORDER BY

- SELECT

- SUM

- WHERE

SQLite3, a database system, can be used. Since Python 2.5, SQLite has been included as part of the package, so if you have Python loaded, it will almost definitely have SQLite.

It will import the findings into a Pandas data frame and make it easier to view our results in an easy-to-read format by using Python to run our SQL code. It also means that we can do more research and visualization with the data we get from the database, but it is beyond the reach of this topic.

If we do not want to use or install Python, you can use the command line to run SQLite3. Simply import the "precompiled binaries" from the SQLite3 website and open the database with the following code:

```
~$ sqlite hubway.db SQLite version 3.14.0 2016-07-26 15:17:14Enter ".help" for usage hints.sqlite>
```

We may simply type in the question we want to run, and the results will appear in our terminal window.

Connecting to the SQLite database using Python is an option to using the terminal. This will enable us to choose a Jupyter notebook to see the effects of our queries in a nicely formatted table.

To accomplish this, we'll create a function that accepts your query (which is processed as a string) as an input and returns a formatted data frame:

```python
import sqlite3
import pandas as pd
db = sqlite3.connect('hubway.db')
def run_query(query):
    return pd.read_sql_query(query,db)
```

3.2 SELECT

SELECT is the first command we'll use. SELECT will be at the heart of virtually every question we write; it informs the server which columns we want to look at. We may specify columns by name (comma is used to separate) or use the wildcard * to return all of the table's columns.

We must say the database which table to get the columns from compared to the columns you want to retrieve. To do so, we use the FROM keyword followed by the table's name. E.g., we could use the following question to see the **bike number** and **start date** for each **trip** in the trips table:

```
SELECT start_date, bike_number FROM trips;
```

When writing SQL queries, it's necessary to remember that any question should end with a semicolon (;). While not every SQL database needs it, some do, so it's a good habit to get into.

3.3 LIMIT

LIMIT is the next command we need to learn before starting running questions on our Hubway database. LIMIT merely instructs the database to return a certain number of rows.

The SELECT question we looked at in the previous part would return the required information for every row in the trips table, but this might result in many details in some cases. We do not like anything. Instead, we might apply LIMIT to our question to see just the **bike number** and **start date** during the first five trips in the database:

```
SELECT start_date, bike_number FROM trips LIMIT 5;
```

We simply inserted the **LIMIT** command followed by a number indicating how many rows we want to be returned. We used 5 in this example, but you can use any number to get the right amount of data for your working task.

In this example, we'll use **LIMIT** a lot in our questions on the Hubway database — the trips table includes over 1.5 million rows of data, and we don't need to see them all!

Let's use the Hubway database to execute our first questionnaire. We'll save our question as a string first, then run it on the database using the function we described earlier. Consider the following scenario:

```
query = 'SELECT * FROM trips LIMIT 5;'
run_query(query)
```

	id	duration	start_date	start_station	end_date	end_station	bike_number	sub_type	zip_code	birth_date	gender
0	1	9	2011-07-28 10:12:00	23	2011-07-28 10:12:00	23	B00468	Registered	'97217	1976.0	Male
1	2	220	2011-07-28 10:21:00	23	2011-07-28 10:25:00	23	B00554	Registered	'02215	1966.0	Male
2	3	56	2011-07-28 10:33:00	23	2011-07-28 10:34:00	23	B00456	Registered	'02108	1943.0	Male
3	4	64	2011-07-28 10:35:00	23	2011-07-28 10:36:00	23	B00554	Registered	'02116	1981.0	Female
4	5	12	2011-07-28 10:37:00	23	2011-07-28 10:37:00	23	B00554	Registered	'97214	1983.0	Female

Instead of naming columns to return, this question uses the wildcard *. This indicates that the **SELECT** command returned every column from the trips table. The **LIMIT** function was also used to limit the contribution to the first five lines of the table.

People always capitalize command keywords in queries (a convention we'll stick to in this guide), but this is more a matter of personal preference. The capitalization allows the code easy to read, but it has little impact on how the code functions. The queries would always run correctly if you choose to write them in lowercase commands.

Any column in the trips table was returned in the previous case. We might overwrite the wildcard with the column names if we were only involved in the period and start date columns:

```
query = 'SELECT duration, start_date FROM trips LIMIT 5'
run_query(query)
```

	duration	start_date
0	9	2011-07-28 10:12:00
1	220	2011-07-28 10:21:00
2	56	2011-07-28 10:33:00
3	64	2011-07-28 10:35:00
4	12	2011-07-28 10:37:00

3.4 ORDER BY

ORDER BY is the last command we need to learn before resolving the first of our questions. We may use this command to filter the database by a certain column.

To use it, all we have to do is decide the name of the column we want to sort on. ORDER BY sorts in increasing order by default. If we choose to define the order for the database, we can use the keywords ASC to increase order and DESC to decrease order.

For instance, we might consider the following line to our question to order the trips table from shortest to longest duration:

```
ORDER BY duration ASC
```

Now that we have the Choose, LIMIT, and ORDER BY commands under our belts, we can try to answer our first question: How long was the longest trip?

It's easier to answer this question if we split it down into parts and figure out which commands we'll need for each one.

To begin, we must extract data from the trips table's period column. Then we will arrange the period column in decreasing order to see which trip is the longest. Here is how we should think about it to come up with a question that returns the details we need:

- Use SELECT to extract the period column FROM the trips table.

- Use ORDER BY to filter the duration column and specify that you want to sort in decreasing order using the Dec keyword.

- Use LIMIT to limit the production to one row.

Using these commands would return the single row with the longest length, providing us with the response to our query.

Another point to keep in mind is that as the questions grow in complexity and include more instructions, you can easily read them if you split them into several lines. This is a matter of personal interest, much like capitalization. It has little effect on how the code works (the machine just reads the code from beginning to end before it meets the semicolon), making the questions more readable. Using triple quote marks in Python, we can divide a string into multiple lines.

Let's put this question to the test and see how long the longest trip lasted.

```
query = '''
SELECT duration FROM trips
ORDER BY duration DESC
LIMIT 1;
'''

run_query(query)
```

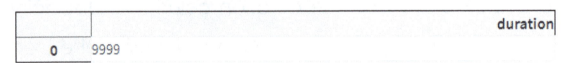

		duration
0	9999	

We now realize that the longest journey lasted 9999 seconds or just more than 166 minutes. We don't know if the overall value of 9999 represents the duration of the largest event or if the database was just set up to make a four-digit number.

If the database is still cutting short especially long trips, we might expect a lot of trips at 9999 seconds until they hit the max. To see if that's the case, run the same question as before, but change the LIMIT to return the ten longest durations:

```
query = '''
SELECT durationFROM trips
ORDER BY duration DESC
LIMIT 10
'''

run_query(query)
```

	duration
0	9999
1	9998
2	9998
3	9997
4	9996
5	9996
6	9995
7	9995
8	9994
9	9994

There aren't many trips at 9999, so it doesn't seem like we're cutting off the upper end of our durations, but it's also hard to say if it's the actual length of the trip or only the highest permitted value.

Hubway charges premium costs on rides longer than 30 minutes (keeping a bike for 9999 seconds would cost an estimated $25 in fees), so it's possible they thought four digits would be enough to manage the bulk of rides.

3.5 WHERE

The former commands are great for getting sorted information for individual columns, but what if we just want to look at a subset of the data? That's where the word WHERE comes into play. The WHERE command helps one to define which rows must be returned using a logical operator. You may, for example, use the command prompt to get a list of all trips taken with bike B00400:

```
WHERE bike_number = "B00400"
```

In this query, you'll also find that we use question marks. Since the bike number is stored as a string, this is the case. Quote, marks would not be needed if the column represented numeric data types.

Let's write a question that returns each column in the trips table for every row with a length greater than 9990 seconds, using the WHERE operator:

```
query = '''
SELECT * FROM trips
WHERE duration > 9990;
'''

run_query(query)
```

	id	duration	start_date	start_station	end_date	end_station	bike_number	sub_type	zip_code	birth_date	gender
0	4768	9994	2011-08-03 17:16:00	22	2011-08-03 20:03:00	24	B00002	Casual			
1	8448	9991	2011-08-06 13:02:00	52	2011-08-06 15:48:00	24	B00174	Casual			
2	11341	9998	2011-08-09 10:42:00	40	2011-08-09 13:29:00	42	B00513	Casual			
3	24455	9995	2011-08-20 12:20:00	52	2011-08-20 15:07:00	17	B00552	Casual			
4	55771	9994	2011-09-14 15:44:00	40	2011-09-14 18:30:00	40	B00139	Casual			
5	81191	9993	2011-10-03 11:30:00	22	2011-10-03 14:16:00	36	B00474	Casual			
6	89335	9997	2011-10-09 02:30:00	60	2011-10-09 05:17:00	45	B00047	Casual			
7	124500	9992	2011-11-09 09:08:00	22	2011-11-09 11:55:00	40	B00387	Casual			
8	133967	9996	2011-11-19 13:48:00	4	2011-11-19 16:35:00	58	B00238	Casual			
9	147451	9996	2012-03-23 14:48:00	35	2012-03-23 17:35:00	33	B00550	Casual			
10	315737	9995	2012-07-03 18:28:00	12	2012-07-03 21:15:00	12	B00250	Registered	'02120	1964	Male
11	319597	9994	2012-07-05 11:49:00	52	2012-07-05 14:35:00	55	B00237	Casual			
12	416523	9998	2012-08-15 12:11:00	54	2012-08-15 14:58:00	80	B00188	Casual			
13	541247	9999	2012-09-26 18:34:00	54	2012-09-26 21:21:00	54	T01078	Casual			

As can be shown, this question yielded 14 separate journeys, each lasting at least 9990 seconds. The fact that all but one of the results has a subtype of "Casual" stands out for this question. Perhaps this indicates that "Registered" consumers are more mindful of the additional costs associated with longer trips. Perhaps Hubway should do a better job explaining its price policy to casual customers to prevent overage fees.

We can see how even a basic understanding of SQL can assist us in answering market questions and uncovering insights from our results.

Restoring to WHERE, we can use AND or OR to combine various logical checks in our WHERE clause. If, for example, we only needed to return trips with a length of over 9990 seconds and a subtype of Registered in our previous question, we could use AND define all conditions.

Another guideline based on personal preference: use parentheses to divide each logical test, as seen in the code block below. Although parentheses aren't specifically necessary for the code to work, they do make the questions easier to understand as they become more complex.

Let's put the question to the test right now. We already know it can only return one answer, so double-checking that we've got it right should be simple:

```
query = '''
SELECT * FROM trips
WHERE (duration >= 9990) AND (sub_type = "Registered")
ORDER BY duration DESC;
'''

run_query(query)
```

	id	duration	start_date	start_station	end_date	end_station	bike_number	sub_type	zip_code	birth_date	gender
0	3157379995		2012-07-03 18:28:00	12	2012-07-03 21:15:00	12	B00250	Registered	'02120	1964.0	Male

"How registered users took many trips?" is the next question we posed at the start of this section. To find an answer, we might use the same question as before, but change the WHERE statement to return all rows with sub-type equal to 'Registered,' and then count them.

However, SQL has a built-in command called COUNT that will do the counting for us.

COUNT helps one transfer the measurement to the spreadsheet without writing extra scripts to count up the output. To use it, simply substitute COUNT(column name) for (or in addition to) the lines you want to Choose, as seen below:

```
SELECT COUNT(id)
FROM trips
```

It makes no difference which column we count in this case since each column should have details for each row in our questionnaire. However, certain rows in a query may have absent (or "null") values. If we're unsure if a column holds null values, we can use the COUNT function on the id column, which is never null because we know our count won't skip anything.

To count every row in our question, we may use COUNT (1) and COUNT (*). It's worth remembering that we would want to run COUNT on a column with null values on occasion. We would like to know how many lines in our database have incomplete data for a column, for example.

Let's look at a query and see how it will help us resolve our issue. We may use SELECT COUNT (*) to sum the total amount of rows returned, and WHERE sub type = "Registered" to confirm that only Listed users' trips are counted.

```
query = '''
SELECT COUNT(*)FROM trips
WHERE sub_type = "Registered";
'''

run_query(query)
```

	COUNT(*)
0	1105192

This query was successful, and the answer to our question was returned. However, the column title isn't really precise. If you showed this table to anyone else, they would have no idea what it meant. If we want to make our output more understandable, we can use AS to create an alias for it (or nickname). Rerun the previous query, except this time use the Total alias Works by Registered Users for our column heading:

```
query = '''
SELECT COUNT(*) AS "Total Trips by Registered Users"
FROM trips
WHERE sub_type = "Registered";
'''

run_query(query)
```

	Total Trips by Registered Users
0	1105192

3.6 Aggregate Functions

SQL has more than one mathematical trick up its sleeves, and COUNT is not merely one. AVG, SUM, MAX and MIN can also get the average, sum, maximum and minimum of a column, respectively. These functions, as well as COUNT, are known as aggregate functions.

Then we can use the AVG feature on the duration column to address our next question, **"What was the average trip duration?"** (and, yet again, using AS to assign our output column a far more descriptive title or name):

```
query = '''
SELECT AVG(duration) AS "Average Duration"
FROM trips;
'''

run_query(query)
```

	Average Duration
0	912.409682

The average trip time turns out to be 912 seconds or around 15 minutes. This makes sense, given that Hubway charges more for trips lasting more than 30 minutes. The service is intended for passengers who only need to make one-way journeys.

Let us look at the next question: do register or casual (non-registered) users travel for longer periods? We know one way of addressing this question: running two **SELECT AVG (period) FROM trips** queries, one for "Registered" users and the other for "Casual" users.

But why not try it a bit differently. The GROUP BY command in SQL can also be used to address that issue in a single query.

3.7 GROUP BY

GROUP BY categorizes rows depending on the contents of a specific column, allowing one to execute aggregate functions on every group.

Take a glance at the gender column to get a better understanding of how this happens. The gender column in each row may have one of three values: "Female," "Male," or Null (missing; the casual users we do not have gender details for).

As we use GROUP BY, the database would divide each row into a different group depending on the **gender** column's value, similar to dividing a stack of cards into individual suits. Imagine having two stacks, one for the males and the other for the females.

Once we have our two distinct stacks, the database will run certain aggregate functions in the query on each one separately. For instance, when we use COUNT, the query will count the total rows in each stack and value every pile individually.

Let us look at how to generate a query to determine which type of users take longer trips, registered or casual.

- As we have for all our previous queries, we will begin with SELECT to inform the database of which data we want to see. We will need sub_type and AVG (period) in this case.

- We will also use GROUP BY term for sub_type to divide our data by subscription category and quantify averages for both registered and casual users individually.

This is how the code appears once it's all put together:

```
query = ...
SELECT sub_type, AVG(duration) AS "Average Duration"
FROM trips
GROUP BY sub_type;
...

run_query(query)
```

	sub_type	Average Duration
0	Casual	1519.643897
1	Registered	657.026067

This shows a big difference! Registered users take trips that last about 11 minutes on average, while casual users spend twice, around 25 minutes per ride. Registered users are most likely taking shorter, more regular rides, perhaps as part of an everyday drive to work. Casual users, however, use up roughly double as much time on each journey.

Casual users likely show up from demographics interested in taking longer rides to ensure they see what there is to see(for example, tourists). Once we have found this variation in the results, there are a variety of aspects the company should look at and learn more about what's the reason behind it.

However, for the sake of this example, let's move on. The next question was, "Which bike was used the most?" We can address this with a query that is quite similar. Evaluate the following example to see how you can find out what each line does — we'll guide you through everything line by line so you can double-check your work:

```
query = '''
SELECT bike_number as "Bike Number", COUNT(*) AS "Number of Trips"
FROM trips
GROUP BY bike_number
ORDER BY COUNT(*) DESC
LIMIT 1;
'''

run_query(query)
```

	Bike Number	Number of Trips
0	B00490	2120

As you may have concluded from the results, bike B00490 was the one that made the most trips. Let's take a look at how we got here:

- The first line is just a SELECT clause informing the database that we need to see the bike_number column and a count of each row. It also employs AS to instruct the database to give each column a more descriptive name.

- The second line specifies that the information we are searching for seems to be within the trips table by using FROM.

- Things tend to get somewhat complicated in the third line. We ask the COUNT function in line 1 to count through every value for bike_number individually using GROUP BY.

- The ORDER BY clause inline-four sorts the table in descending order, ensuring that the most used bike will be at the top.

- Finally, we use LIMIT to restrain the output to the very first row, which, based on how we grouped the data on line four, we know would be the bike that was used in the most trips.

3.8 Arithmetic Operators

The last question is considerably more difficult than the others. We'd like to see the average time the registered users over the age of 30 spent on their trips.

We might estimate the year that 30-year-old users were born in our minds and insert it in. Still, a more sophisticated approach is by using arithmetic operations effectively within our query. The SQL operators +, -, *, and / can execute an arithmetic operation on a whole column in one go.

```
query = '''
SELECT AVG(duration) FROM trips
WHERE (2017 - birth_date) > 30;
'''

run_query(query)
```

	AVG(duration)
0	923.014685

3.9 JOIN

We have only been focused on queries that extract information out of the trips table so far. One of several reasons why SQL is so efficient is that it enables us to extract information from multiple tables simultaneously.

A second table, named **stations**, is included in our bike-sharing database. The stations' table has an **id column** linked to the **trips** table, which gives every station inside the Hubway network.

Let us revisit the theoretical order tracking database mentioned before while heading to some actual examples from this database. We had two tables in that database: **orders** and **customers**, linked by the **customer_id** column.

Let us assume we needed to create a query that would return the **order_number** and **name** for each order inside the database. We might use the following question if they were all put in the same table:

```
SELECT order_number, name
FROM orders;
```

Because the order number and name columns are located in two separate tables, we must perform a few additional steps. Let's take a minute to consider what else the database would need to remember so it can retrieve the details we're looking for:

- In which table the order_number column is present?

- In which table the name column is present?

- What is the relationship between the information in the orders table and the customers' table?

We should add the table names for every column in the SELECT command to address the first two questions. We do this by simply writing the table and column names divided by a '.'. For instance, we will write **SELECT orders. Order number, customers. Name** rather than writing **SELECT order number, name**. Writing the table names is a way of asking the database which table to search for each column. It will help the database locate the columns we are searching for.

We use JOIN and ON to inform the database of the connection of **orders** and **customers** tables. ON identifies which columns in every table are associated, and JOIN determines which tables must be linked.

We use an inner join, which implies that rows will be obtained only if the columns listed in ON match. In this case, we'll use JOIN on any tables that weren't included in the FROM function. Therefore we can use one of the following:

- **FROM customers INNER JOIN orders**

- **FROM orders INNER JOIN customers**

These tables are linked by the **customer_id** column inside each table, as we mentioned earlier. As a result, we'll use ON to inform the database that both these columns apply to the same thing, as seen below:

```
ON orders.customer_ID = customers.customer_id
```

We use the '.' once more to ensure that the database identifies which table each of these columns belongs to. So, when we place it all together, we get the following query:

```
SELECT orders.order_number, customers.name
FROM orders
INNER JOIN customers
ON orders.customer_id = customers.customer_id
```

This query would provide the order number for each order in the database and the customer name affiliated with that order.

We can now write few queries in our Hubway database to see how JOIN works.

Have a look through the remaining columns within the **station** table before we get started. Here's a query that will display the first five rows of the **station's** table so we can know what it looks like:

```
query = '''
SELECT * FROM stations
LIMIT 5;
'''

run_query(query)
```

id	station	municipality	lat	lng
0 3	Colleges of the Fenway	Boston	42.340021	-71.100812
1 4	Tremont St. at Berkeley St.	Boston	42.345392	-71.069616
2 5	Northeastern U / North Parking Lot	Boston	42.341814	-71.090179
3 6	Cambridge St. at Joy St.	Boston	42.361284999999995	-71.06514
4 7	Fan Pier	Boston	42.353412	-71.044624

- **id** — Each station's unique identifier (relates to the columns in the trips table, **start_station** and **end_station**)

- station — The name of the station

- municipality — The city or town where the station is located (Brookline, Boston, Somerville or Cambridge)

- **lat** — The station's latitude

- lng — The station's longitude

- Which are the most common stations for round trips?

- How many trips begin and conclude in various municipalities?

We'll attempt to answer some questions in the details, beginning with "Which is the most common station for round trips as a starting point?" Let's take it one move at a time:

- **SELECT** is used first to get the station column out of the stations' table. To get several rows, **COUNT** will also be used.

- Next, using **JOIN**, the database will be asked to connect the specific tables **ON** the **id** column in the **stations**' table and the start_**station** column in the **trips** table.

- Then we get down to business, **GROUPING BY** the station column in the stations' column so that our COUNT can count the number of trips for each station individually.

- Finally, we can ORDER BY COUNT and LIMIT the number of results to a manageable number.

```
query = '''
SELECT stations.station AS "Station", COUNT(*) AS "Count"
FROM trips INNER JOIN stations
ON trips.start_station = stations.idGROUP BY stations.stationORDER BY COUNT(*) DESC
LIMIT 5;
'''

run_query(query)
```

		Station	Count
0	South Station - 700 Atlantic Ave.		56123
1	Boston Public Library - 700 Boylston St.		41994
2	Charles Circle - Charles St. at Cambridge St.		35984
3	Beacon St / Mass Ave		35275
4	MIT at Mass Ave / Amherst St		33644

You'll realize why these are the most popular stations if you're familiar with Boston. Charles Street runs along the river near some nice scenic roads, and Boylston and Beacon streets are located downtown with several office buildings, and South Station is one of the city's major commuter rail stations. What stations are most commonly used for round trips is the next topic we'll look at. We may use the same question that we used before. We'll SELECT the same output columns and JOIN the tables the same way we did before, except this time we'll add a WHERE clause to limit our COUNT to trips where the **start_station** and **end_station** are the same.

```
query = '''SELECT stations.station AS "Station", COUNT(*) AS "Count"
FROM trips INNER JOIN stations
ON trips.start_station = stations.id
WHERE trips.start_station = trips.end_station
GROUP BY stations.station
ORDER BY COUNT(*) DESC
LIMIT 5;
'''

run_query(query)
```

	Station	Count
0 The Esplanade - Beacon St. at Arlington St.		3064
1 Charles Circle - Charles St. at Cambridge St.		2739
2 Boston Public Library - 700 Boylston St.		2548
3 Boylston St. at Arlington St.		2163
4 Beacon St / Mass Ave		2144

As can be seen, many of these stations are similar to those in the previous issue, but the numbers are significantly smaller. The busiest stations remain the busiest stations, but the lower overall figures show that people are more likely to use Hubway bikes to get from source to destination instead of cycling around for a while before returning to their starting point. There is one notable difference: the Esplanade, which was not among the busiest stations overall in our previous query, now appears to be the busiest for round trips.

The following question is: how many trips begin and end in various municipalities? This question goes a little further. We'd like to know how many trips begin and end in various cities. To do so, we must twice JOIN the trips table to the stations' table.

ON the **start station** column once and ON the **end station** column twice. To accomplish this, we must construct an alias for the station table to distinguish between data about the start station and data about the end station. We can accomplish this using AS in the same way we've been developing aliases for individual columns to give them a more intuitive name. For example, we can use the following code to JOIN the **stations**' table to the **trips** table using an alias of 'start.' We can then combine 'start' with our column names. To refer to data that comes from this specific JOIN (rather than the second JOIN we will do ON the **end_station** column):

```
INNER JOIN stations AS start ON trips.start_station = start.id
```

When we run the query, this is what it would look like. We've used the symbol > to indicate "is not equivalent to," but!= could also be used.

```
query =
...
SELECT COUNT(trips.id) AS "Count"
FROM trips INNER JOIN stations AS start
ON trips.start_station = start.id
INNER JOIN stations AS end
ON trips.end_station = end.id
WHERE start.municipality <> end.municipality;
...

run_query(query)
```

		Count
0	309748	

This means that about 300,000 (or 20%) of the 1.5 million trips ended in a different municipality than where they began, indicating that people prefer to use Hubway bicycles for short trips rather than longer trips between cities. Congratulations, if you've managed it this far! You've started learning the fundamentals of SQL. We've gone through the CHOOSE, GROUP BY, LIMIT, ORDER BY, WHERE, and JOIN commands, as well as cumulative and arithmetic functions. These will provide you with a solid base upon which to develop as you progress on your SQL journey.

Chapter 4 – Make Your Own SQL Database

4.1 Install and Set Up SQL

SQL Server databases are among the most widely used databases, owing to their ease of development and maintenance. You will not have to fumble around with the command line if you use a free graphical user interface (GUI) software like SQL Server Management.

Step 1: Set up SQL.

a. Make sure you are using the right version.

b. Select New SQL Server stand-alone setup from the drop-down menu.

c. Have all new product details.

d. In Selecting Features, Instance Setup, and Server Configuration, accept the defaults.

e. Choose Mixed Mode under Authentication Mode in Database Engine Configuration.

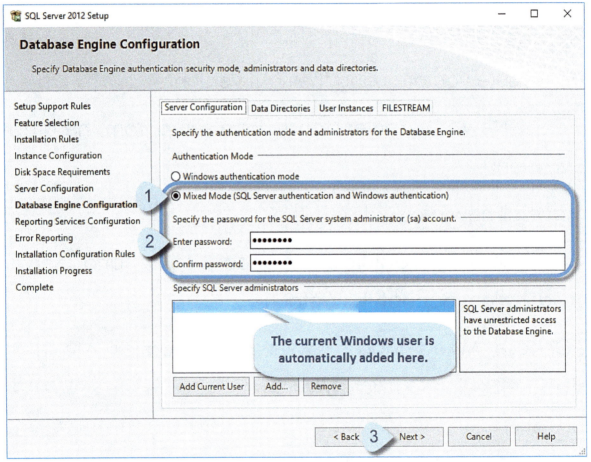

2. For your website, build a SQL database.

a. Open the Sql Management Studio software on your device.

b. Right-click Databases in the Object Manager panel and select New Database.

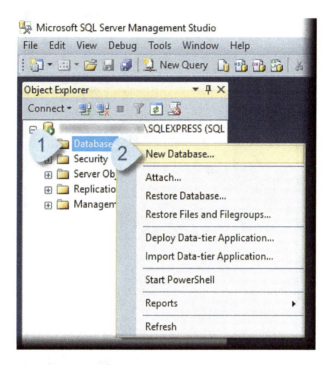

a.   Write the new database name and then click OK.

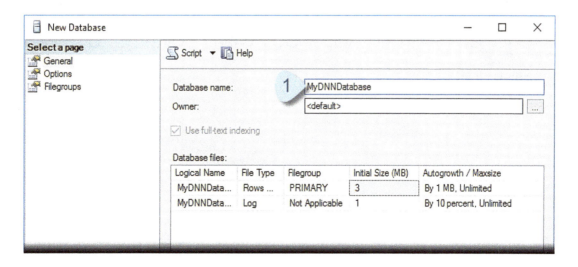

Remember or Write down the database name for further use.

2.   Create a user account of SQL.

a.   Under **Security tab**, choose **New Login** by right-clicking on **Logins.**

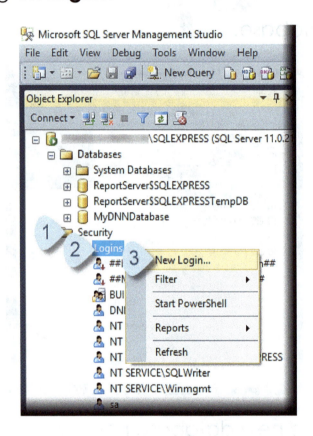

b.   Select SQL Server encryption, enter a password, uncheck the box Apply password policy, and select the database.

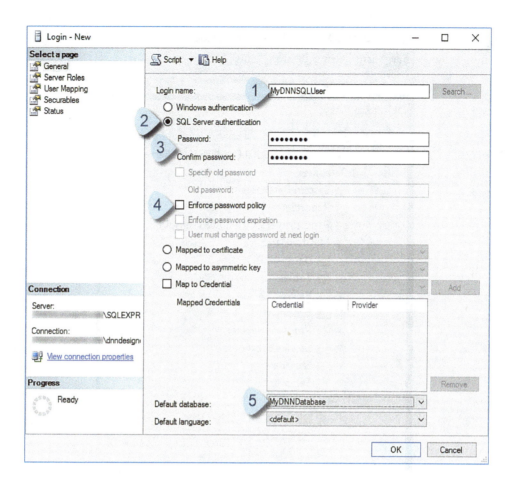

Remember or write down the login requirements for further use in DNN.

3. Grant access to the current database to the new SQL administrator db owner.

a. Right-click on Users in the Object Explorer panel, below your database > Security, and choose New User.

b. Choose SQL user with username as the user class.

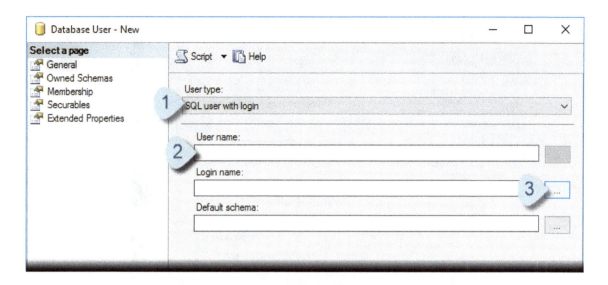

a. Enter the login information for and then tap check names as shown in figure below.

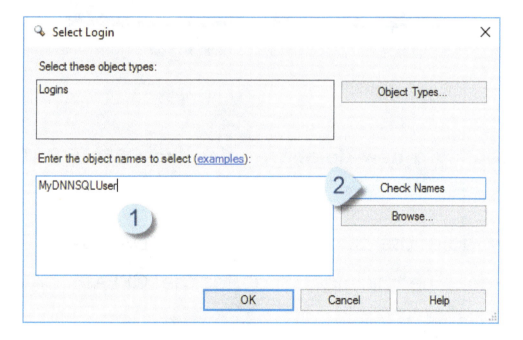

b. Select Membership from Under Select a page, and tap the db_owner database part membership.

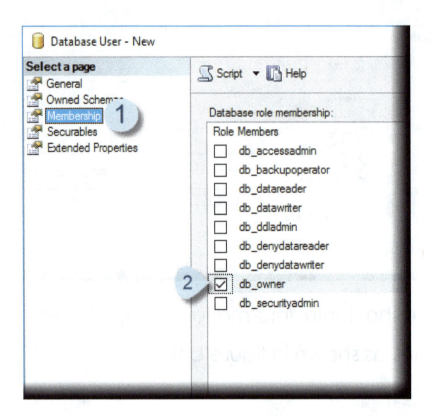

4.2 Creating a new database using the CREATE DATABASE statement

A new database is created with the DATABASE CREATE argument. The minimal syntax for the CREATE DATABASE declaration is as follows:

```
CREATE DATABASE database_name;
```

The database name is defined after CREATE DATABASE word in this syntax.

Inside a SQL Server case, the database title must be special. It also has to follow the SQL Server identifier's guidelines. The database name is usually limited to 128 characters.

The sentence below generates a new database called TestDb:

```
CREATE DATABASE TestDb;
```

The newly generated database can be used in the Object Explorer until the assertion has been successfully executed. If the new application does not show, you can refresh the object list by pressing F5 on your keyboard.

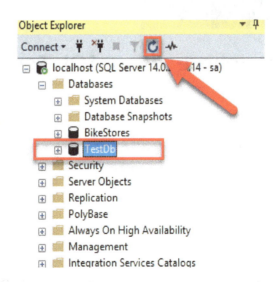

This statement shows all records in the SQL Server:

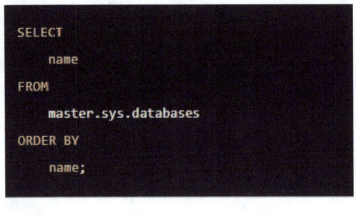

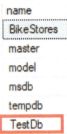

Or you can run the program **sp_databases**:

```
EXEC sp_databases;
```

4.3 Creating a Database Using SQL Server Management Studio

This topic explains how to use Sql Server to build a database in SQL Server.

Requirements

The CREATE DATABASE argument must be executed in auto commit mode (the standard transaction management mode), and it is not permitted to be executed in an overt or implied transaction.

Observations and suggestions

• Any time a user database is generated, updated, or dropped; the master database must be backed.

Make the data files as wide as possible when creating a database, depending on the maximum number of data you anticipate in the database.

to construct a database

1. Bind to a Sql Database Engine instance in Object Explorer and then extend the instance.

2. Right-click Databases, then choose New Database from the drop-down screen.

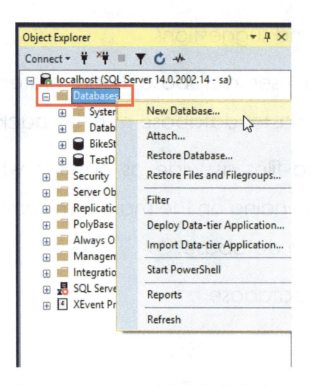

Click the OK button after entering a domain name, such as
SampleDb, in New Database.

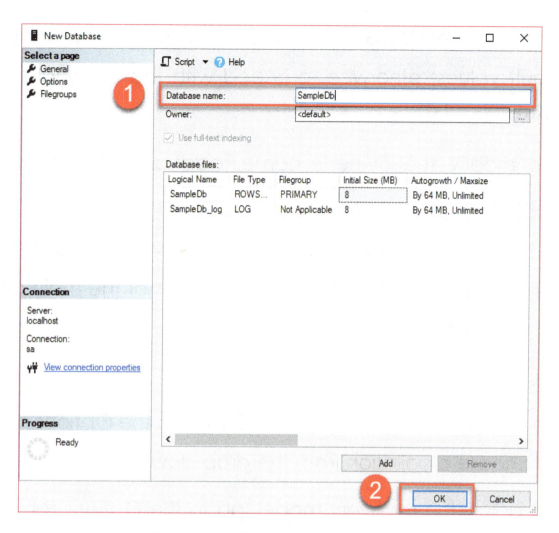

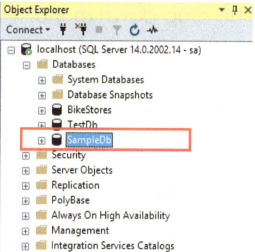

1 Click OK after step 3 to build the database by approving all default values; otherwise, proceed with the optional steps below.

2. To modify the owner's name, add another owner by clicking (...).

3. In the Database files grid, select the relevant cell and enter the new value to adjust the existing values of the main data and application log files.

4. To adjust the database's collation, go to the Options page and choose a collation from the drop-down menu.

5. To adjust the recovery model, go to the Options tab and choose one from the drop-down menu.

6. To switch database settings, go to the Options page and update the database options there.

7. Go to the Filegroups tab to create a new filegroup. After clicking Add, fill in the filegroup's values.

Click the Expanded Properties page to apply an enhanced property to the index.

9. Give the expanded property a name in the Name column.

10. Type the expanded property text in the Value column. Enter one or more sentences that define the database, for example.

11. Click OK to build the database.

4.4 Creating a Database Using Transact-SQL

To construct a database

1. Provide a link to the database engine.

2. Choose New Query from the Standard bar.

3. Paste the following sample into the question window and press the Execute button. The database Sales were created in this case. The first file (Sales dat) becomes the main file since the keyword PRIMARY is not used. Since the Main character for the Sales dat file does not specify MB or KB, it requires MB and is reserved in megabytes. Since the MB suffix is expressly specified in the SIZE parameter, the Sales log file is reserved in megabytes.

```
USE master ;
GO
CREATE DATABASE Sales
ON
( NAME = Sales_dat,
    FILENAME = 'C:\Program Files\Microsoft SQL Server\MSSQL13.MSSQLSERVER\MSSQL\DATA\saledat.mdf',
    SIZE = 10,
    MAXSIZE = 50,
    FILEGROWTH = 5 )
LOG ON
( NAME = Sales_log,
    FILENAME = 'C:\Program Files\Microsoft SQL Server\MSSQL13.MSSQLSERVER\MSSQL\DATA\salelog.ldf',
    SIZE = 5MB,
    MAXSIZE = 25MB,
    FILEGROWTH = 5MB ) ;
GO
```

Chapter 5 – Mistakes to Avoid with SQL

SQL programming can be both enjoyable and frustrating. Traditional programming languages like Java, C, C++, and VB have a hard time adapting to the "set-based" mentality. Also, veteran SQL developers as well as DBAs will fall victim to one of the SQL language's many pitfalls. It takes time to master the fundamentals, and even then, certain errors are difficult to find.

The aim of this section would be to illustrate a few of the more frequent errors that people have been making while programming SQL. The list is based on the experience interacting with various production teams and engineers, doing code reviews, and so on, and also the problems seen on newsgroups and forums on a daily basis. The following list of typical blunders is by no means complete, and it is listed in no specific order of severity.

Here is the list, without further ado:

- The NOT IN predicate and NULLs

- Predicates of functions on indexed columns

- The subquery column is incorrect.

- Predicate data form mismatch

- The order in which the variables are evaluated is called the predicate evaluation order.

- Predicate placement and outer joins

- Subqueries that return several results

- Use of SELECT *

- User-defined scalar functions

- Excessive use of cursors

The examples are written in the Transact-SQL dialect of SQL Server, but the definitions are applicable to any SQL implementation.

5.1 NULLs and the NOT IN predicate

One of the most frequent requests is for data to be retrieved based on a column value that is not in a set of values. The situation is depicted in the following two charts. Tables with various colors and items are available:

Colors table:

```
color
----------
Black
Blue
Green
Red
Products table:
sku   product_description   color
----  --------------------  ------
1     Ball                  Red
2     Bike                  Blue
3     Tent                  NULL
```

Please keep in mind that these tables do not reflect a flawless template that adheres to normalization rules and best practices. Instead, it is a condensed case to further explain the point. In fact, the colors table will almost certainly have a color code main column that the goods table would refer to.

The request is to choose from a selection of colors that have not been used on a commodity before. To put it another way, we need to create a question that only returns colors for which there are no products.

At first glance, the NOT IN predicate seems to have a very intuitive plan to meet this order, one that is very similar to how the problem will be expressed in plain English:

```sql
SELECT C.color
FROM Colors AS C
WHERE C.color NOT IN (SELECT P.color
                      FROM Products AS P);
```

You might expect this question to display two rows (for 'black' and 'green,' respectively), but it instead returns a blank result set:

```
color
----------

(0 row(s) affected)
```

This is obviously wrong. What exactly is the issue? The presence of NULL, that is not a value however a marker to signify lost (or UNKNOWN) knowledge, drives SQL's three-valued logic. In the IN predicate, as the NOT operator is added to the set of values from its subquery, it is interpreted as follows:

```
"color NOT IN (Red, Blue, NULL)"
```

This is the same as:

```
"NOT(color=Red OR color=Blue OR color=NULL)"
```

The sentence "color=NULL" evaluates to UNKNOWN, and NOT UNKNOWN also evaluates to UNKNOWN according to the laws of three-valued logic. As a consequence, the question returns a null set since all rows have been filtered out.

As conditions change and a non-nullable column is changed to accept NULLs, this error is common. It also emphasizes the importance of rigorous research. And if a column is designed to not accept NULLs, you can double-check that your queries still function for NULLs.

Because EXISTS uses two-valued predicate logic that evaluates to TRUE/FALSE, one alternative is to use it instead of IN:

```
SELECT C.color
FROM Colors AS C
WHERE NOT EXISTS(SELECT *
                 FROM Products AS P
                 WHERE C.color = P.color);
```

This question yields the predicted range of results:

```
color
----------
Black
Green
```

The following are some other options:

```
/* IS NOT NULL in the subquery */
SELECT C.color
FROM Colors AS C
WHERE C.color NOT IN (SELECT P.color
                      FROM Products AS P
                      WHERE P.color IS NOT NULL);

/* EXCEPT */
SELECT color
FROM Colors
EXCEPT
SELECT color
FROM Products;

/* LEFT OUTER JOIN */
SELECT C.color
FROM Colors AS C
LEFT OUTER JOIN Products AS P
  ON C.color = P.color
WHERE P.color IS NULL;
```

Although all solutions achieve the desired outcomes, EXCEPT to be the simplest to comprehend and implement. It is worth noting that the EXCEPT operator produces distinct values, which is perfect in our case but may not be the case in another.

5.2 Functions on indexed columns in predicates

We tend to write code as though it were a direct translation of a request. If we are asked to extract all customers whose names begin with the letter L, for example, it feels normal to write the question as follows, by using LEFT function to display the very first letter of their names:

```
SELECT customer_name
FROM Customers
WHERE LEFT(customer_name, 1) = 'L';
```

Alternatively, if we are asked to quantify overall revenue for January 2009, we could use the DATEPART feature to remove the appropriate month as well as year from the sale date list, as seen below:

```
SELECT SUM(sale_amount) AS total_sales
FROM Sales
WHERE DATEPART(YEAR, sale_date) = 2009
  AND DATEPART(MONTH, sale_date) = 1;
```

While these queries seem to be straightforward, you will notice that the indexes on the customer's name and sale date columns are not being used, and the execution schedule for these queries reveals index scans.

The issue occurs because the index columns are transferred to a function, that the query engine then has to validate for each and every row in the table. The WHERE clause predicate is considered "non-SARGable" in these situations, and the question optimizer's best option is to do a complete index or table search.

We must stop using functions upon on indexed columns to ensure that the indexes are included. Rewriting the queries in our two cases to use SARG-able predicates is a surprisingly easy process. This logically similar question can be used to express the first request:

```
SELECT customer_name
FROM Customers
WHERE customer_name LIKE 'L%';
```

For the second question, the equivalent is as follows:

```
SELECT SUM(sale_amount) AS total_sales
FROM Sales
WHERE sale_date >= '20090101'
  AND sale_date <  '20090201';
```

To extract the data easily and reliably, these two queries are more likely to use index seek.

It is important to note that SQL Server is becoming "smarter" as time goes by. Consider the question below, which employs the CAST function on the indexed sale date column:

```
SELECT SUM(sale_amount) AS total_sales
FROM Sales
WHERE CAST(sale_date AS DATE) = '20090101';
```

You will see an index search if you execute this query on SQL 2005 or earlier. Despite the use of the CAST feature, SQL Server 2008 will perform an index seek. The predicate is translated into something like this, according to the implementation plan:

```
SELECT SUM(sale_amount) AS total_sales
FROM Sales
WHERE sale_date >= '20090101'
  AND sale_date <  '20090102';
```

However, rather than relying on the optimizer's changing intelligence, you can use SARGable predicates wherever possible.

5.3 Incorrect subquery column

It is very simple to detach yourself from the key question logic and focus only on the subquery while composing a subquery. This may contribute to the unintentional substitution of a column from its subquery source table for a column from the main query with a similar name.

Let us take a look at two very basic tables: one contains revenue statistics, while the other is an auxiliary Calendar table that contains both calendar dates and holidays (abbreviated here):

Sales table:

```
sale_date   sale_amount
----------  -----------
2009-01-01  120.50
2009-01-02  115.00
2009-01-03  140.80
2009-01-04  100.50
```

Calendar table:

```
calendar_date  holiday_name
-------------  ----------------
2009-01-01     New Year's Day
2009-01-02     NULL
2009-01-03     NULL
2009-01-04     NULL
2009-01-05     NULL
```

Our task is to collect sales data for specific holiday dates. It appears to be a simple question to construct:

```sql
SELECT sale_date, sale_amount
FROM Sales AS S
WHERE sale_date IN (SELECT sale_date
                    FROM Calendar AS C
                    WHERE holiday_name IS NOT NULL);
```

The question, on the other hand, clearly returns all rows from the Sales table! A closer examination of the question shows that the SELECT list of the subquery is to blame. It incorrectly refers to the Sales table's sales date column rather than the Calendar table's calendar date column.

Why didn't we get a mistake if that is the case? About the fact that the result was not what we had hoped for, this is indeed a true SQL assertion. The columns of the outer query are revealed to the inner query by using a subquery. We inadvertently transformed the self-contained subquery, which was supposed to be executed once and the value forwarded to the outer query, into a correlated subquery, which was supposed to be logically executed once with each row returned by the outer query.

As a response, the subquery compares to sale date IN (sale date), which is only valid if the Calendar table has at least one holiday date, and our result collection includes all rows from the Sales table. Of course, in this case, the solution is straightforward: we actually use the right date column from its Calendar table:

```sql
SELECT sale_date, sale_amount
FROM Sales AS S
WHERE sale_date IN (SELECT C.calendar_date
                    FROM Calendar AS C
                    WHERE C.holiday_name IS NOT NULL);
```

Another relevant point is that prefixing columns in subqueries with table aliases is a best technique. For eg, if only we had used the following alias:

```sql
SELECT sale_date, sale_amount
FROM Sales AS S
WHERE sale_date IN (SELECT C.sale_date
                    FROM Calendar AS C
                    WHERE holiday_name IS NOT NULL);
```

The question would have returned an error stating, "Error: Invalid column name'sale date'."

5.4 Data type mismatch in predicates

This is another common blunder that can be difficult to spot. In predicates, it is very simple to mix up data types. It may be in a stored procedure in which the parameter is transferred as one data type and used in a query to sort data on another data type column. Another example is joining tables based on various data types in columns, or just using a predicate where data types are misaligned.

For eg, suppose we have a Customers table with a VARCHAR last name column:

```
CREATE TABLE Customers (
  customer_nbr INT NOT NULL PRIMARY KEY,
  first_name VARCHAR(35) NOT NULL,
  last_name VARCHAR(35) NOT NULL);
```

Then, to extract consumer information by last name, the following stored protocol is used:

```
CREATE PROCEDURE GetCustomerByLastName
  @last_name NVARCHAR(35)
AS
  SELECT first_name, last_name
  FROM Customers
  WHERE last_name = @last_name;
```

It is worth noting that the parameter @last name is of the NVARCHAR data form. Although the code seems to run, SQL

Server would have to convert the last name column to NVARCHAR implicitly because NVARCHAR has higher data precedence. A results penalty can be imposed as a result of this. The implied conversion is labeled CONVERT IMPLICIT in the question schedule. A data type mismatch can also prevent the need for an index seek, depending on the collation and other considerations. The dilemma is solved by using the right data type:

```
CREATE PROCEDURE GetCustomerByLastName
 @last_name VARCHAR(35)
AS
 SELECT first_name, last_name
 FROM Customers
 WHERE last_name = @last_name;
```

This error is often the product of team members sharing tasks, with one designing tables and the other implementing stored procedures or coding. Another explanation may be that when joining data from separate data sources, the join columns in the source structures contain different data forms. The same recommendation extends not only to character data type mismatches, but to numeric data type mismatches (such as INT and FLOAT) and numeric and character data type combining.

5.5 Predicate evaluation order

If you are familiar with logical database processing order, you may assume a query to be performed in this order:

- FROM

- WHERE

- GROUP BY

- HAVING

- SELECT

The preceding sequence depicts the sequential order in which queries should be executed. The FROM clause, which defines the source data set, is processed first, followed by the WHERE predicates, GROUP BY, and so on.

Physically, however, the query is handled differently, and the query optimizer is free to transfer expressions around in the query plan to find the most cost-effective way to retrieve the results. As a result, many people believe that a buffer in the WHERE clause is added before the subsequent steps are processed. A predicate will, in effect, be used much later in the physical execution schedule. Predicates are often executed in no particular order, from left to right. If you have a WHERE clause that says, "WHERE x=1 AND y=2," for example, there's no guarantee that "x=1" will be evaluated first. They will be carried out in any order.

Consider the following Accounts table, where Business accounts are represented by a numeric reference as well as Personal accounts by a character reference in the account reference column:

```
account_nbr  account_type      account_reference
-----------  ---------------   -----------------
1            Personal          abc
2            Business Basic    101
3            Personal          def
4            Business Plus     5
```

This chart, in general, suggests poor architecture. The account reference column should be split into two distinct attributes, one for company accounts and the other for personal accounts, each with the appropriate data form (not belonging to the similar table). In reality, though, we often have to work with programs that have flaws and where changing the specification is not a choice.

A legitimate request in the above situation is to recover all company style accounts with an account reference greater than 20. (assuming account reference contain some useful numeric value for business type accounts). This is an example of a query:

```sql
SELECT account_nbr, account_reference AS account_ref_nbr
FROM Accounts
WHERE account_type LIKE 'Business%'
  AND CAST(account_reference AS INT) > 20;
```

The query, however, returns an error:

```
Conversion failed when converting the varchar value 'abc' to data type int'
```

The question fails because, as previously said, there is no set order in which predicates must be evaluated, and nothing ensures that the predicate "account type LIKE 'Business percent'" will be assessed before the predicate "CAST (account reference AS INT) > 20." The second predicate is checked first in our case, leading in a conversion error for personal accounts due to incorrect values in the account reference list.

One possible solution is to utilize a derived table (or common table expression) to search the company type accounts first, then add the account reference column predicate:

```sql
SELECT account_nbr, account_ref_nbr
FROM (SELECT account_nbr,
             CAST(account_reference AS INT) AS account_ref_nbr
      FROM Accounts
      WHERE account_type LIKE 'Business%') AS A
WHERE account_ref_nbr > 20;
```

However, since derived tables and CTEs are extended in the query plan and then a single query plan is made, predicates may be moved up or down in the plan again, this results in the same error.

As previously said, the issue is a combination of poor implementation and a misconception of how SQL Server executes physical queries. What is the answer? The only approach is to properly plan the table and avoid keeping mixed data in one column. A workaround in this case is to use a CASE statement to ensure that only correct numeric values are translated to the INT data type:

```sql
SELECT account_nbr, account_reference AS account_ref_nbr
FROM Accounts
WHERE account_type LIKE 'Business%'
  AND CASE WHEN account_reference NOT LIKE '%[^0-9]%'
          THEN CAST(account_reference AS INT)
      END > 20;
```

The CASE expression checks for correct numeric values using a LIKE pattern (a double negation logic is used, which can be interpreted as "there is not a specific level that is not a digit"), and only executes the CAST for those values. The CASE expression returns NULL for the remaining values, which is filtered out since NULL is not matched for any value (even with NULL).

5.6 Outer joins and placement of predicates

Outer joins are a fantastic feature, but they are often overlooked and manipulated. Some users seem to enjoy them enough that they include one in almost every question, even though it is not needed!

Understanding the logical steps taken to process an outer join in a query is crucial to proper use of outer joins. The following are the steps from the query processing processes that are relevant:

- For the two input tables in the FROM clause, a cross join (Cartesian product) is formed. Any possible combination of a row from the first table as well as a row from the second table is the consequence of the Cartesian product.

- The ON clause predicates are used to process the data, resulting in only rows that satisfy the predicate logic.

- Any Outer rows that were filtered out in step 2 by the predicates are re-added. The preserved table's rows are added with their current attribute values (column values), while the non-preserved table's attributes (columns) are set to NULL.

- The predicates of the WHERE clause are included.

Depending about how you write an outer join question and where you put predicates in it, you will get entirely different outcomes. Let us take a look at a scenario based on the two tables below, Customers and Orders:

Customers table:

```
customer_nbr  customer_name
------------  -------------
1             Jim Brown
2             Jeff Gordon
3             Peter Green
4             Julie Peters
```

Orders table:

```
order_nbr    order_date  customer_nbr order_amt
----------   ----------  ------------ ----------
1            2008-10-01  1            15.50
2            2008-12-15  2            25.00
3            2009-01-02  1            18.00
4            2009-02-20  3            10.25
5            2009-03-05  1            30.00
```

Our task is to obtain a list of all clients, as well as the overall amount spent on orders, that since beginning of 2009. One could write the following question on the spur of the moment:

```sql
SELECT C.customer_name, SUM(COALESCE(O.order_amt, 0)) AS total_2009
FROM Customers AS C
LEFT OUTER JOIN Orders AS O
   ON C.customer_nbr = O.customer_nbr
WHERE O.order_date >= '20090101'
GROUP BY C.customer_name;
```

However, the findings are not encouraging:

```
customer_name    total_2009
--------------   -----------
Jim Brown          48.00
Peter Green        10.25
```

Clientele Jeff and Julie are not included in the list of results. What exactly is the issue? Let us take a look at this query one stage at a time, following the logical processing order, and see what went wrong. A cross link between the 2 input tables is the first step:

```sql
SELECT C.customer_name, O.order_amt
FROM Customers AS C
CROSS JOIN Orders AS O;
```

As a consequence, any possible row combination from both input tables appears:

```
customer_name       order_amt   order_date
----------------    ---------   ----------
Jim Brown            15.50      2008-10-01
Jim Brown            25.00      2008-12-15
Jim Brown            18.00      2009-01-02
Jim Brown            10.25      2009-02-20
Jim Brown            30.00      2009-03-05
Jeff Gordon          15.50      2008-10-01
Jeff Gordon          25.00      2008-12-15
Jeff Gordon          18.00      2009-01-02
Jeff Gordon          10.25      2009-02-20
Jeff Gordon          30.00      2009-03-05
Peter Green          15.50      2008-10-01
Peter Green          25.00      2008-12-15
Peter Green          18.00      2009-01-02
Peter Green          10.25      2009-02-20
Peter Green          30.00      2009-03-05
Julie Peters         15.50      2008-10-01
Julie Peters         25.00      2008-12-15
Julie Peters         18.00      2009-01-02
Julie Peters         10.25      2009-02-20
Julie Peters         30.00      2009-03-05
```

The ON predicates of a JOIN clause are then applied:

```
SELECT C.customer_name, O.order_amt, O.order_date
FROM Customers AS C
INNER JOIN Orders AS O
   ON C.customer_nbr = O.customer_nbr;
```

This question returns only customers that have placed orders. Customer Julie is not included in the outcome set because she has no orders:

```
customer_name   order_amt   order_date
-------------   ---------   ----------
Jim Brown        15.50      2008-10-01
Jeff Gordon      25.00      2008-12-15
Jim Brown        18.00      2009-01-02
Peter Green      10.25      2009-02-20
Jim Brown        30.00      2009-03-05
```

The outer rows are added back in the third stage of the logical processing order. Since the join predicates were not satisfied in the previous stage, these rows were omitted.

```
SELECT C.customer_name, O.order_amt, O.order_date
FROM Customers AS C
LEFT OUTER JOIN Orders AS O
   ON C.customer_nbr = O.customer_nbr;
```

Julie has now been re-added to the result set. Notice how the preserved table's outer rows (Customers) have values for the chosen attributes (customer name), while the non-preserved table's outer rows (Orders) have NULL for their attributes (order amt and order date):

```
customer_name    order_amt    order_date
-------------    ---------    ----------
Jim Brown        15.50        2008-10-01
Jim Brown        18.00        2009-01-02
Jim Brown        30.00        2009-03-05
Jeff Gordon      25.00        2008-12-15
Peter Green      10.25        2009-02-20
Julie Peters     NULL         NULL
```

The final step is to use the predicates in the WHERE clause:

```
SELECT C.customer_name, O.order_amt, O.order_date
FROM Customers AS C
LEFT OUTER JOIN Orders AS O
   ON C.customer_nbr = O.customer_nbr
WHERE O.order_date >= '20090101';
```

The photo is now clear! The WHERE clause predicate is to blame. Customer Jeff is filtered out of the result set because he has no orders after January 1, 2009, and customer Julie is sorted out as she has no orders at all (because the order date section in the outer row applied for Julie is NULL). In this scenario, the WHERE clause's predicate effectively converts the outer join to an inner join.

It is enough to switch the WHERE predicate into the join state to fix our original question.

```
SELECT C.customer_name, SUM(COALESCE(O.order_amt, 0)) AS total_2009
FROM Customers AS C
LEFT OUTER JOIN Orders AS O
  ON C.customer_nbr = O.customer_nbr
 AND O.order_date >= '20090101'
GROUP BY C.customer_name;
```

Since Jeff and Julie are sorted out of the join predicates, but afterwards added back as the outer rows are added, the question now returns valid results.

```
customer_name   total_2009
-------------   ----------
Jeff Gordon     0.00
Jim Brown       48.00
Julie Peters    0.00
Peter Green     10.25
```

In a more complicated scenario involving multiple joins, incorrect filtering can occur on a corresponding table operator (such as a join to some other table) rather than in the WHERE clause. Let us assume we get an OrderDetails table with product SKUs and quantities, and the request is to have a list of all consumers, along with order amounts and quantities, for a set of product SKUs. The following question could seem to be correct:

```sql
SELECT C.customer_name, O.order_amt, D.qty
FROM Customers AS C
LEFT OUTER JOIN Orders AS O
  ON C.customer_nbr = O.customer_nbr
INNER JOIN OrderDetails AS D
  ON D.order_nbr = O.order_nbr
 AND D.sku = 101;
```

The INNER join with the OrderDetails table, on the other hand, performs the same function as the predicate in the WHERE clause in our prior trial, effectively converting the LEFT OUTER join to an INNER join. To answer this request, the right query must use a LEFT OUTER add to connect to the OrderDetails table:

```sql
SELECT C.customer_name, O.order_amt, D.qty
FROM Customers AS C
LEFT OUTER JOIN Orders AS O
  ON C.customer_nbr = O.customer_nbr
LEFT JOIN OrderDetails AS D
  ON D.order_nbr = O.order_nbr
 AND D.sku = 101;
```

5.7 Subqueries that return more than one value

The retrieval of a value based on any association with the key query table is a very common request. Take into account the following tables, which store information about goods and the plants that produce them:

Products table:

```
sku     product_description
-----   ------------------
1       Bike
2       Ball
3       Phone
```

Product Plants table:

```
sku     plant_nbr
-----   -----------
1       1
2       1
3       2
```

The order is for each product's processing plant to be extracted. To retrieve the vine, one way to fulfill the requirement is to submit the following query utilizing correlated subquery:

```
SELECT sku, product_description,
      (SELECT plant_nbr
       FROM ProductPlants AS B
       WHERE B.sku = A.sku) AS plant_nbr
FROM Products AS A;
```

It is important to remember that the aim here is to demonstrate a technique; there might be a more effective way to complete the same task. However, everything goes smoothly, and we will have the expected results:

```
sku   product_description plant_nbr
----  ------------------- -----------
1     Bike                1
2     Ball                1
3     Phone               2
```

The question would happily run until the day comes that the corporation wishes to start producing Balls at Plant 3 in order to meet increased demand. This is how the Product Plants table now looks:

```
sku    plant_nbr
-----  -----------
1      1
2      1
2      3
3      2
```

Suddenly, our question begins to return the following error:

Msg 512, Level 16, State 1, Line 1

More than one value was returned by the subquery. Whether the subquery is followed by =, =,,=, >, >=, or if the subquery is being used as a verb, this is not allowed.

The mistake is sufficiently descriptive. Our subquery produces a result collection instead of the intended scalar value, which splits the query. The solution is straightforward, given our business needs. We simply choose a JOIN: to list all production plants for a certain commodity.

```
SELECT A.sku, A.product_description, B.plant_nbr
FROM Products AS A
JOIN ProductPlants AS B
  ON A.sku = B.sku;
```

The question now runs smoothly and correctly, returning the following results:

```
sku   product_description   plant_nbr
----  --------------------  ----------
1     Bike                  1
2     Ball                  1
2     Ball                  3
3     Phone                 2
```

The same error will occur in a predicate that tests a column or expression against a subquery, such as "... column = (SELECT value FROM Table) ". In that situation, the IN predicate can be used instead of "=."

5.8 Use of SELECT *

When we first meet SQL, we still applaud the genius who devised the SELECT * syntax! It is extremely convenient and simple to use! Rather than stating all column names directly in our questions, we simply use the magic wildchar '*' to retrieve all columns. A typical example of SELECT * misuse is extracting a set of all plastic items and inserting them into some other table with the same structure:

It is over! However, market needs change from time to time, and two additional columns are attached to the Products table:

```
ALTER TABLE Products
ADD effective_start_date DATETIME,
    effective_end_date DATETIME;
```

Suddenly, the magical query returns an error:

Msg 213, Level 16, State 1, Line 1

Insert Error: Column name or number of supplied values does not match table definition.

The solution is to list the column names directly in the query:

```
INSERT INTO PlasticProducts (sku, product_description, material_type)
SELECT sku, product_description, material_type
FROM Products
WHERE material_type = 'plastic';
```

If a view is generated with **SELECT *** and the base tables are later changed to include or exclude columns, the situation will get even worse.

Note: If the **SCHEMABINDING** option is used to generate a view, the base tables could not be changed in any manner that affects the view description.

Finally, **SELECT *** can never be used in development code! While using the EXISTS predicate, there is one exception. Since only the presence of rows is essential, the selection list in the filename for the EXISTS predicate is ignored.

5.9 Scalar user-defined functions

One of the first things we learn while learning to program in any language is how to reuse code, and SQL is no different. It gives you a lot of options for logically grouping and reusing coding.

The scalar user-defined feature is one such method in SQL Server. It seems too easy to put all those complicated equations into a function and then call it from our queries. However, the "sting in the tail" is that it can have a significant impact on results. Scalar functions are checked for each row if used in a query, which can lead in very slow queries when dealing with large tables. This is particularly valid whenever the scalar function has to extract data from another table.

Here is an illustration. The request is to retrieve gross sales per product from tables containing products and sales for products. Since the net revenue value can be used again elsewhere, you decide to measure total sales for a commodity using a scalar function:

```
CREATE FUNCTION dbo.GetTotalSales(@sku INT)
RETURNS DECIMAL(15, 2)
AS
BEGIN
  RETURN(SELECT SUM(sale_amount)
         FROM Sales
         WHERE sku = @sku);
END
```

The question to get the overall revenue for each commodity will then look something like this:

```
SELECT sku, product_description, dbo.GetTotalSales(sku) AS total_sales
FROM Products;
```

Isn't this a lovely and well-designed query? But wait till you put it to the test on a huge dataset. Each row will have the gross revenue figure repeated, and also the overhead will be equal to the number of rows. If necessary, rewrite the equation as a table-valued function, or perform the calculation directly in the main question. Doing the calculation in the questionnaire in our example would look like this:

```sql
SELECT P.sku, P.product_description, SUM(S.sale_amount) As total_sales
FROM Products AS P
JOIN Sales AS S
  ON P.sku = S.sku
GROUP BY P.sku, P.product_description;
```

Here is a table-valued feature you can use to figure out total sales:

```sql
CREATE FUNCTION dbo.GetTotalSales(@sku INT)
RETURNS TABLE
AS
RETURN(SELECT SUM(sale_amount) AS total_sales
       FROM Sales
       WHERE sku = @sku);
```

The APPLY operator can now be used in the question to call the table-valued function:

```sql
SELECT sku, product_description, total_sales
FROM Products AS P
CROSS APPLY dbo.GetTotalSales(P.sku) AS S;
```

5.10 Overuse of cursors

Let us face it: loops are one of our favorite things. A loop is one of the first structures we experience while learning to program in Visual Basic, C, C++, Java, or C#. They will assist you with about every problem you might have.

As a result, it is only logical to look for our favorite loop build the first time we begin programming with SQL. Here it is the all-powerful cursor (along with its little Bit brother)! And we rush to apply the well-known technique to our problems.

Let us take a look at an example. We must conduct a monthly update of commodity prices given a table with product prices; the price changes are deposited in another table with new prices.

Product Prices table:

sku	price	effective_start_date	effective_end_date
1	10.50	2009-01-01	NULL
2	11.50	2009-01-01	NULL
3	19.00	2009-01-01	NULL
4	11.25	2009-01-01	NULL

New Prices table:

sku	price
2	11.25
4	12.00

The following is an example of a cursor solution:

```sql
DECLARE @sku INT;
DECLARE @price DECIMAL(15, 2);

DECLARE PriceUpdates
CURSOR LOCAL
        FORWARD_ONLY
        STATIC
        READ_ONLY
FOR SELECT sku, price
    FROM NewPrices;

OPEN PriceUpdates;

FETCH NEXT FROM PriceUpdates
        INTO @sku, @price;

WHILE @@FETCH_STATUS = 0
BEGIN

  UPDATE ProductPrices
  SET price = @price,
      effective_start_date = CURRENT_TIMESTAMP
  WHERE sku = @sku;

  FETCH NEXT FROM PriceUpdates
        INTO @sku, @price;

END

CLOSE PriceUpdates;
DEALLOCATE PriceUpdates;
```

The mission has been completed! While the question is going, we can now take a well-deserved rest. Soon, it becomes clear that procedural row-by-row execution in SQL does not work well. Our solution is lengthy, difficult to read, and manage, in addition to being sluggish. This is when we realize how powerful SQL's set-based existence is. A more powerful set-based query that is simple to study and manage will accomplish the same task:

```
UPDATE ProductPrices
SET price = (SELECT N.price
             FROM NewPrices AS N
             WHERE N.sku = ProductPrices.sku),
    effective_start_date = CURRENT_TIMESTAMP
WHERE EXISTS(SELECT *
             FROM NewPrices AS N
             WHERE N.sku = ProductPrices.sku);
```

There are several ways to solve this problem with a set-based query: utilizing the MERGE statement, updating with Common Table Expression, or using the SQL Server-specific update with enter. However, the point is to take advantage of SQL's inherent strength to solve problems using set-based methods rather than procedural solutions.

Although cursors can be avoided wherever possible, there are some issues, such as running complete aggregations, that are still better solved with cursors today. We have reason to believe that potential improvements would have improved resources for solving such challenges in a set-based manner.

Conclusion

SQL stands for Structured Query Language, and it is a programming language used to store, manipulate, and retrieve data from a relational database. The Relational Database System (RDBMS) standard language is SQL.

SQL is the standard database language used by all Relational Database Management Systems (RDMS) such as MySQL, Postgres, Oracle, MS Access, Informix, Sybase, and SQL Server. You will improve your skills and specialize as a programmer, developer, project manager, and more by learning SQL. Knowing SQL makes you a valuable asset in the workplace.

Especially as more and more companies become digitized, and every business journal mentions analytics or business intelligence. If the use of analytics and business intelligence (BI) increases (which it will, as the amount of data grows), so will the demand for data professionals. And SQL is the main skill that will allow you to become the expert that businesses are looking for.

Perhaps now is a good time to do your next SQL code analysis. Hopefully, any of these examples can help you become a better developer/DBA and write more stable and efficient code. These patterns aren't always easy to spot, particularly in more complex queries. However, preventing these errors is simple if you grasp the fundamentals.